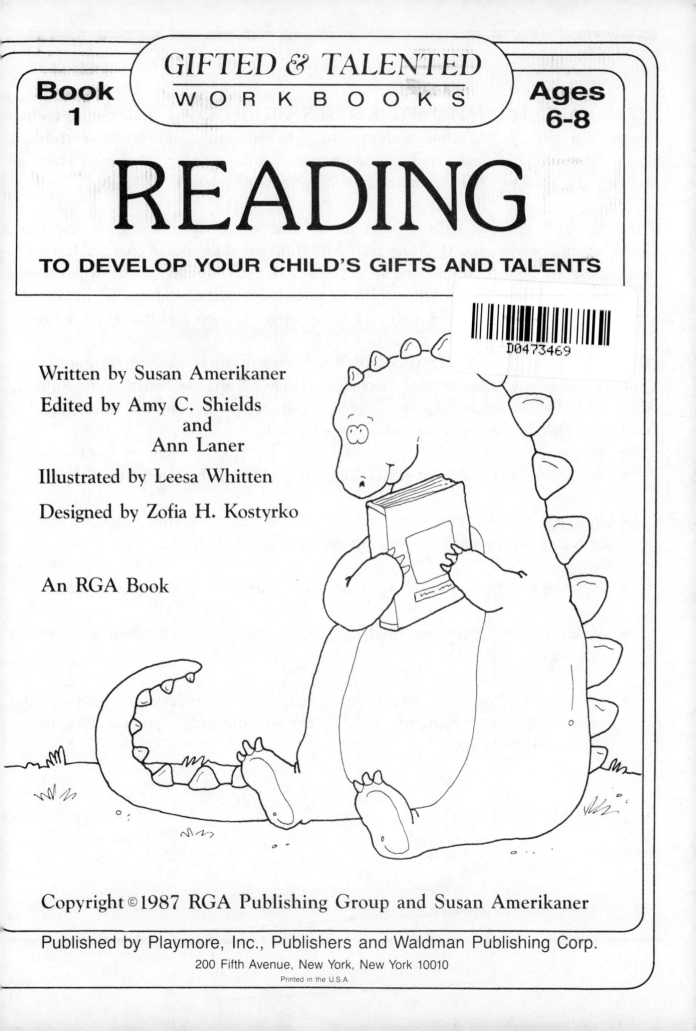

Book 1

GIFTED & TALENTED
W O R K B O O K S

Ages 6-8

READING

TO DEVELOP YOUR CHILD'S GIFTS AND TALENTS

Written by Susan Amerikaner

Edited by Amy C. Shields
and
Ann Laner

Illustrated by Leesa Whitten

Designed by Zofia H. Kostyrko

An RGA Book

Published by Playmore, Inc., Publishers and Waldman Publishing Corp.

200 Fifth Avenue, New York, New York 10010

Printed in the U.S.A.

Note to Parents:

GIFTED AND TALENTED WORKBOOKS will help develop your child's natural talents and gifts by providing activities to enhance critical and creative thinking skills. These skills of logic and reasoning teach children **how** to think. They are precisely the skills emphasized by teachers of gifted and talented children.

Thinking skills are the skills needed to be able to learn anything at any time. Unlike events, words, and teaching methods, thinking skills never change. If a child has a grasp of how to think, school success and even success in life will become more assured. In addition, the child will become self-confident as he or she approaches new tasks with the ability to think them through and discover solutions.

GIFTED AND TALENTED WORKBOOKS present these skills in a unique way, combining the basic subject areas of reading, language arts, and math with thinking skills. The top of each page is labeled to indicate the specific thinking skill developed. Here are some of the skills you will find:

- Deduction – the ability to reach a logical conclusion by interpreting clues

- Understanding Relationships – the ability to recognize how objects, shapes, and words are similar or dissimilar; to classify and categorize

- Sequencing – the ability to organize events, numbers; to recognize patterns

- Inference – the ability to reach logical conclusions from given or assumed evidence

- Creative Thinking – the ability to generate unique ideas; to compare and contrast the same elements in different situations; to present imaginative solutions to problems

How to use GIFTED AND TALENTED WORKBOOKS

Each book contains activities that challenge children. The activities vary in range from easier to more difficult. You may need to work with your child on many of the pages, especially with the child who is a non-reader. However, even a non-reader can master thinking skills, and the sooner your child learns how to think, the better. Read the directions to your child, and if necessary, explain them. Let your child choose to do the activities that interest him or her. When interest wanes, stop. A page or two at a time may be enough, as the child should have fun while learning.

It is important to remember that these activities are designed to teach your child **how to think,** not how to find the right answer. Teachers of gifted children are never surprised when a child discovers a new "right" answer. For example, a child may be asked to choose the object that doesn't belong in this group: a table, a chair, a book, a desk. The best answer is **book,** since all the others are furniture. But a child could respond that all of them belong because they all could be found in an office. The best way to react to this type of response is to praise the child and gently point out that there is another answer too. While creativity should be encouraged, your child must look for the best and most **suitable** answer.

GIFTED AND TALENTED WORKBOOKS have been written and designed by teachers. Educationally sound and endorsed by leaders in the gifted field, this series will benefit any child who demonstrates curiosity, imagination, a sense of fun and wonder about the world, and a desire to learn. These books will open your child's mind to new experiences and help fulfill his or her true potential.

Princess Nancy dreams about a knight in shining armor. Read all about him. Which one of the knights is Nancy dreaming about? Write his name.

He has long, straight hair.
His face is smooth and clean.
His shield has the royal seal.
His name is

_____.

Barry   Lester   Alan   Alberto

4

Who did it? Ms. Riley saw the robber. Read her description. Then write his name below.

"He had curly hair and a scar over his right eye. He had a mustache. He was very thin."

Zak

Sam

Harry

Albert

Ralph

Max

The thief is _____ .

Read all the clues. Then write the name of each girl below her. Make sure you read **all** the clues first!

A.　　　B.　　　C.　　　D.　　　E.

1.　Carol is wearing a hat. She is between Leesa and Joyce.

2.　Alana is not wearing shoes. She is next to Leesa.

3.　Helen is holding a ball.

4.　Where is Joyce?

Six girls are having a pajama party. Read all the clues. Then write each girl's name in the correct place.

A. _____

F. _____

B. _____

E. _____

C. _____

D. _____

1. Susan is across from Hilary.

2. Mary is next to Susan, who is closest to the food.

3. Maria is not next to Mary or Hilary.

4. Jill is having a pillow fight with Maria.

5. Where is Yolanda?

Seven people live in this apartment house. Read all the clues. Then write each person's name in the correct place.

1. Adam loves flowers. He lives on the bottom floor next to Tony.

2. Carl is on the top floor.

3. Carl lives above two boys. One of them is Willy.

4. Sherry lives between Mike and Tony.

5. Where does Sophia live?

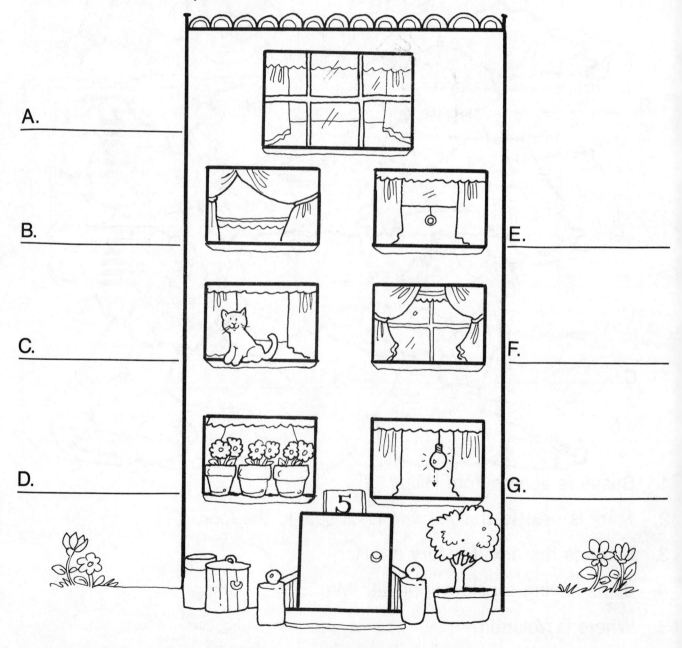

A.

B.

C.

D.

E.

F.

G.

For each number, cross out the one thing that you **don't** need to know:

1. To fix a bike you need to know
   a. what tools to use
   b. what time the bike broke
   c. how a bike works

2. To build a dog house you need to know
   a. the size of the dog
   b. where your tools are
   c. what the dog eats for dinner

3. To go camping you need to know
   a. where your friends camped last summer
   b. the weather report
   c. how to start a fire

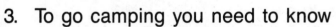

4. To wash the car you need to know
   a. how to hook up the hose
   b. how to drive
   c. where the soap is

For each number, cross out the one thing that you **don't** need to know.

1. To go on vacation you need to know
   a. what time you are going
   b. how big the hotel is
   c. what clothes to pack

2. To make spaghetti you need to know
   a. how to set the table
   b. how many people will be eating
   c. how to boil water

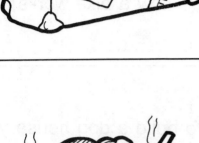

3. To give a book report you need to know
   a. who the author is
   b. what the story is about
   c. who else has read the book

4. To go sailing you need to know
   a. what the sail is made of
   b. how fast the wind is blowing
   c. which way the wind is blowing

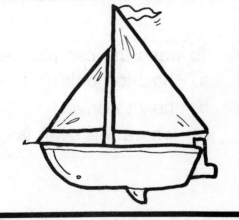

Circle the picture that is the same as the one in the box, but turned in a different way.

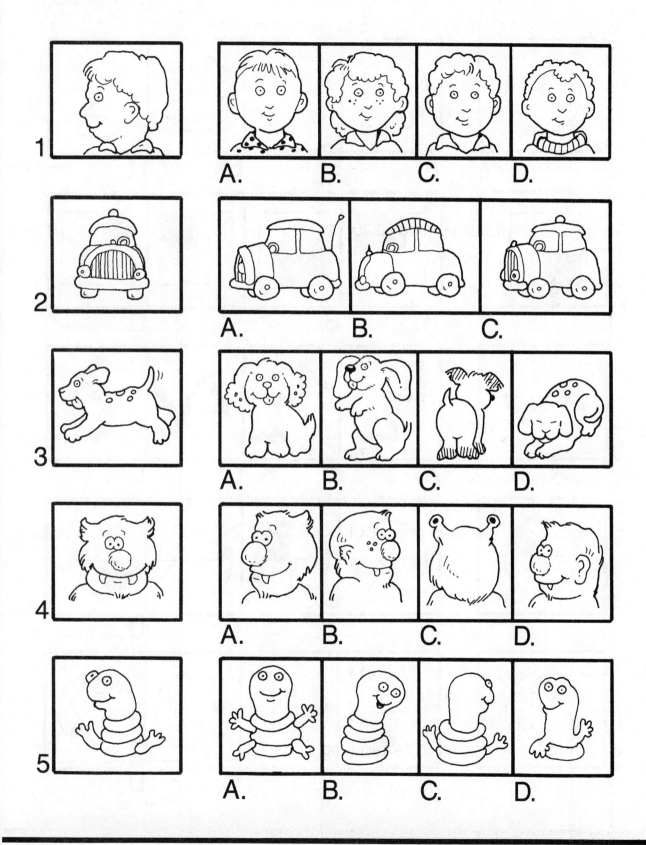

1. A.   B.   C.   D.

2. A.   B.   C.

3. A.   B.   C.   D.

4. A.   B.   C.   D.

5. A.   B.   C.   D.

Circle the picture that is the same as the one in the box, but turned in a different way. The first one is done for you.

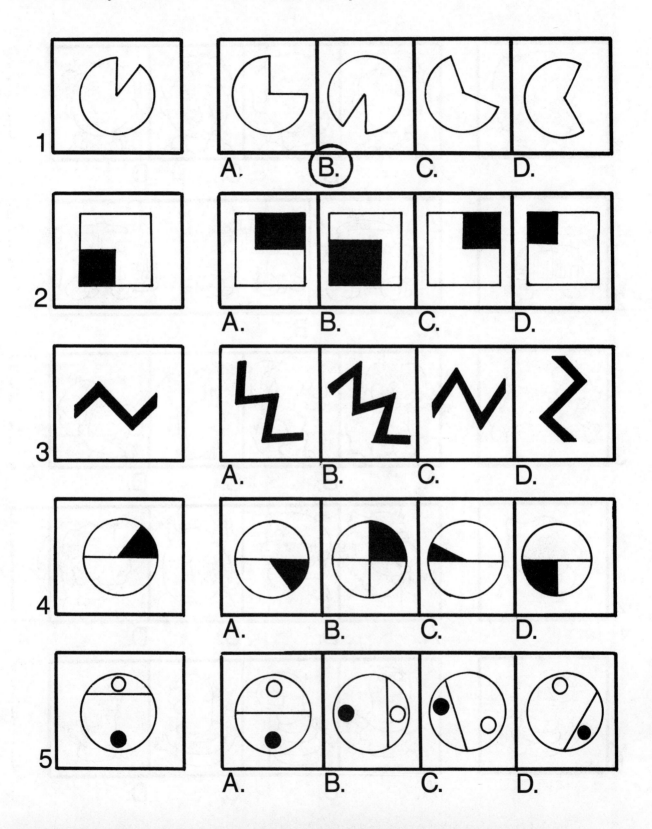

1. A. B. C. D.

2. A. B. C. D.

3. A. B. C. D.

4. A. B. C. D.

5. A. B. C. D.

Circle the picture that is the same as the one in the box, but turned upside-down. The first one is done for you.

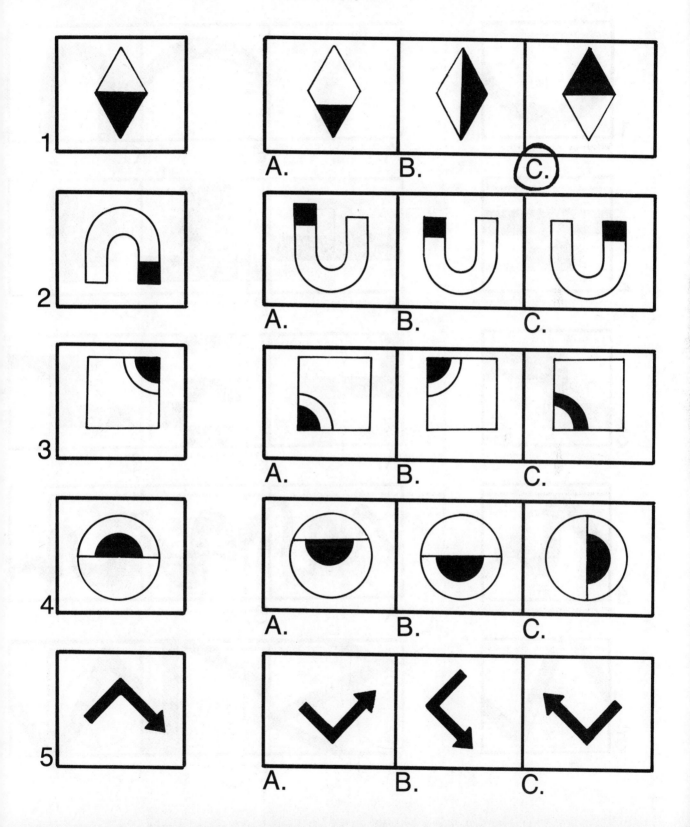

Circle the design that is the same as the first one, but turned upside-down.

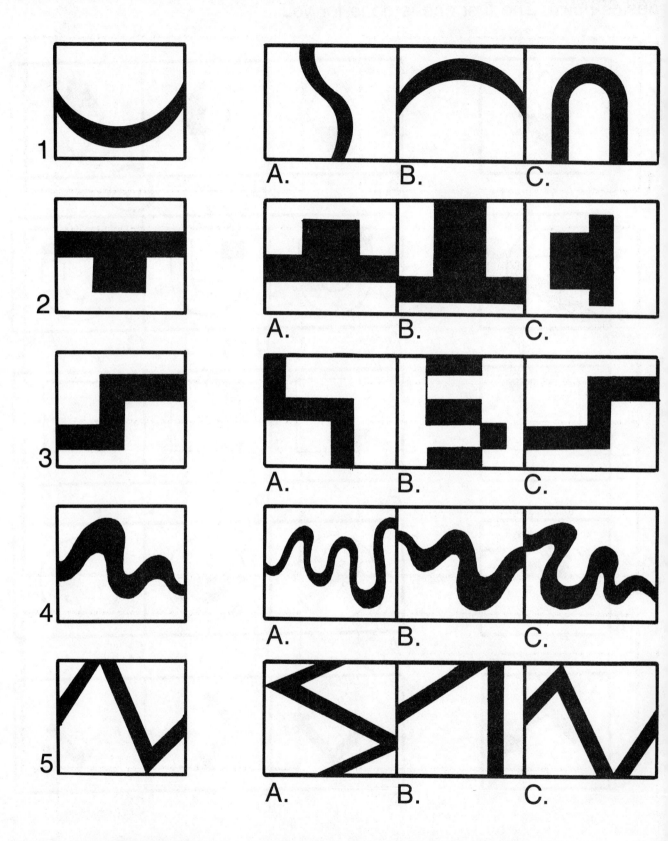

1
    A.   B.   C.

2
    A.   B.   C.

3
    A.   B.   C.

4
    A.   B.   C.

5
    A.   B.   C.

Draw each picture again — but draw it upside-down. Think carefully before you draw!

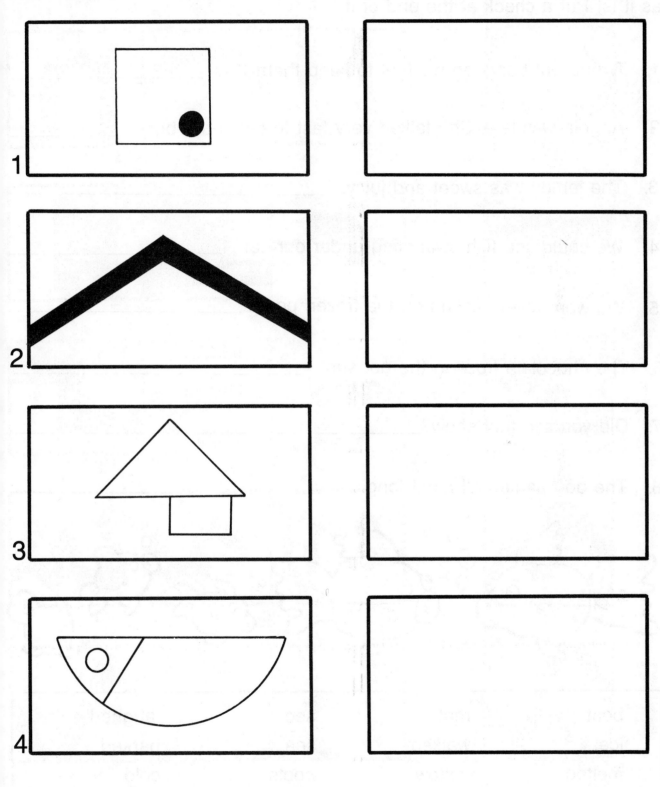

Cross out the incorrect word in each sentence. Find the correct word in the word list and write it at the end of the sentence. **One** sentence is correct just as it is! Put a check at the end of it.

1. Tyrone put boats on his feet to keep them dry. _____

2. Angela was late. She talked very fast to catch the bus. _____

3. The lemon was sweet and juicy. _____

4. We could see fish swimming under our car. _____

5. We went roller skating on the frozen pond. _____

6. The chocolate froze in the hot sun. _____

7. Did you see that show? _____

8. The dog parked all night long. _____

boat	mat	see	laughed
ice	walked	sea	barked
melted	yellow	boots	cold

Cross out the incorrect word in each sentence. Find the correct word in the word list and write it at the end of the sentence. **One** sentence is correct just as it is! Put a check at the end of it!

1. Washington, D.C. is the middle of our country. _____

2. She didn't here a thing I said. _____

3. Ann was smiling. She was sorry she came to the party. _____

4. He walked so fast we couldn't understand him. _____

5. She fell and scraped her knee. _____

6. The fire burned for hours. There was much left of the house. _____
    _____

7. Her parents were proud of her. Her report card was awful. _____

8. She could hear smoke. She knew something was burning. _____

glad	more	top	hear
smell	capital	pet	feel
talked	wasn't	great	green

17

Cross out the incorrect word in each sentence. Find the correct word in the word list and write it at the end of the sentence. **One** sentence is correct just as it is! Put a check at the end of it.

1. Are you crazy? Have you locked your marbles? _____

2. After swimming, she felt dead in one ear. _____

3. We hurried so we wouldn't miss the end of the movie. _____

4. The newspaper was yellow and stiff. It was old. _____

5. She knocked over the milk. Her pants were sold. _____

6. Luisa hit a home run just in time to win the football game. _____

   _____

7. The park opens after dark. _____

8. Larry put on a wool glove to keep his head warm. _____

start	looked	sad	closes
hat	baseball	ear	soaked
lost	deaf	shoe	tennis

18

Princess Roxanne has a lot to do today before she goes to the Wizard for her magic lesson. She made a list of errands, but they are not in the right order. Number her errands in the best order so she can get to the Wizard's house on time.

A. _____ Pick up her computer.

B. _____ Buy nails to repair castle doors.

C. _____ Kill the dragon.

D. _____ Buy food for the alligators in the moat.

E. _____ Get cake for the royal feast.

19

Mr. Smith has many errands to do before he goes to work at the bank today. Number the errands in the best order so he can get to work on time.

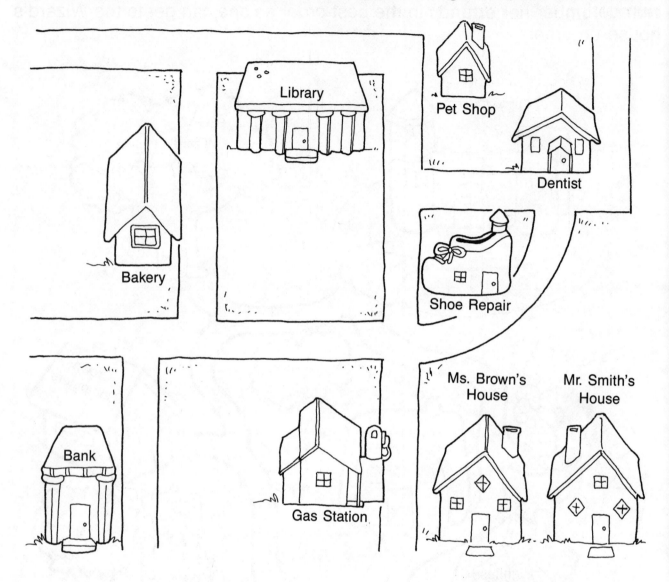

A. ＿＿＿ Return library books.

B. ＿＿＿ Pick up his shoes.

C. ＿＿＿ Buy bread.

D. ＿＿＿ Get gas.

E. ＿＿＿ Borrow sugar from Ms. Brown.

F. ＿＿＿ Get his teeth cleaned.

20

Red Riding Hood and the Wolf are both going to visit Grandma, but their directions are all mixed up. Put their directions in order by numbering them from 1 to 3.

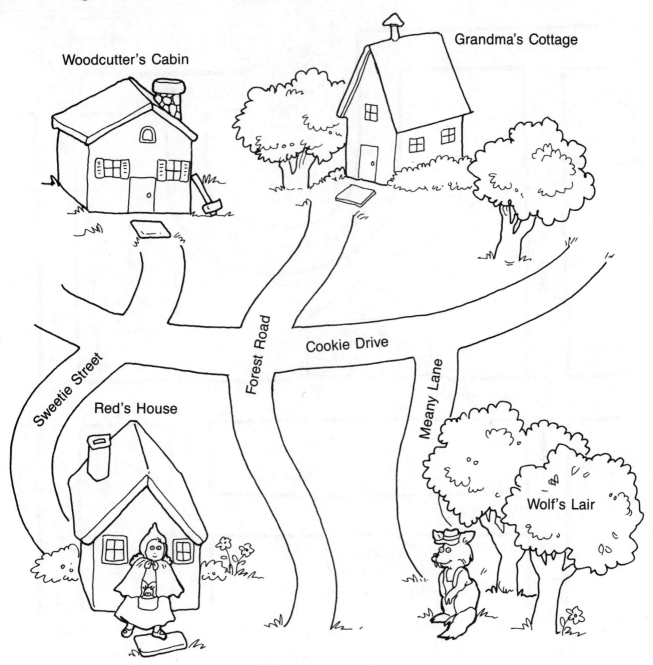

Red

A. _____ Make a left on Forest Road.

B. _____ Walk up Sweetie Street.

C. _____ Go right at Cookie Drive.

Wolf

A. _____ Go up Meany Lane.

B. _____ Go right at Forest Road.

C. _____ Go left at Cookie Drive.

Sam and Dan are going to the market. Their directions are mixed up. Put their directions in order by numbering from 1 to 4.

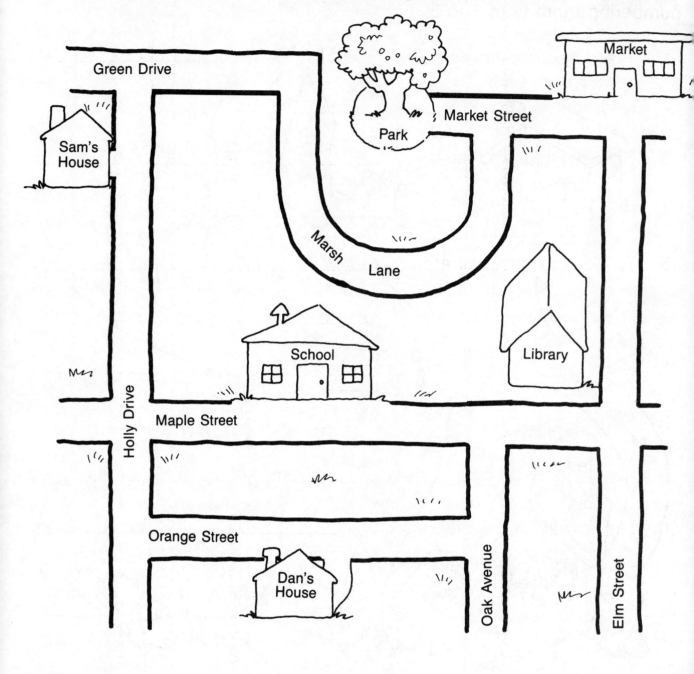

Sam

A.____ Go right on Marsh Lane.

B.____ Go right on Market Street.

C.____ Go left on Holly Drive.

D.____ Go right on Green Drive.

Dan

A.____ Go right on Maple Street.

B.____ Go left on Elm Street.

C.____ Make a left on Oak Avenue.

D.____ Go right on Orange Street.

How is each pair of words alike? Use the word bank to complete each sentence. The first one has been done for you.

1. Grass and lettuce are __green__ .

2. Red and yellow are _____ .

3. Bananas and apples are _____ .

4. Houses and castles are _____ .

5. Tennis and baseball are _____ .

6. Computers and cars are _____ .

7. Hammers and rulers are _____ .

8. Kittens and puppies are _____ .

9. Amy and Susan are _____ .

10. Hurricanes and tornadoes are _____ .

salty	green	cars	girls
sports	hats	machines	buildings
storms	fruits	tools	slow
babies	clothes	colors	

How is each pair of words alike? Use the word bank to complete each sentence.

1. Snow and cotton are _____ .

2. Birds and kites _____ .

3. Wheels and records _____ .

4. Children and hair _____ .

5. Mexico and France are _____ .

6. London and Paris are _____ .

7. Doors and windows _____ .

8. Spring and fall are _____ .

9. Mark and Adam are _____ .

10. Balloons and feathers are _____ .

light	heavy	lakes	go around
seasons	boys	countries	fly
grow	open	cities	shows
run fast	hot	white	

How is each pair alike and different? The first one is done for you.

A unicorn and a cow

Alike: _____ They both have four legs. _____

Different: _____ The unicorn has one horn. _____

unicorn

cow

A circle and a square

Alike: _____

Different: _____

A castle and an igloo

Alike: _____

Different: _____

A turtle and a seahorse

Alike: _____

Different: _____

How is each pair alike and different?

A bed and a chair

Alike: _____

Different: _____

Milk and soda pop

Alike: _____

Different: _____

Skin and grass

Alike: _____

Different: _____

Crying and laughing

Alike: _____

Different: _____

Read each sentence. Think how the first pair of things go together. Use the word bank to complete the sentence and make the second pair of things go together **in the same way** as the first pair. The first one is done for you.

1. Boots are to feet as gloves are to _____**hands**_____.

2. Puppy is to dog as kitten is to _____.

3. Finger is to hand as toe is to _____.

4. Bird is to nest as cow is to _____.

5. Thursday is to Friday as May is to _____.

6. Coat is to closet as car is to _____.

7. Apple is to fruit as rose is to _____.

8. Milk is to drink as meat is to _____.

road	June	April	garage
cat	hands	ring	barn
eat	flower	mother	foot

Read each sentence. Think how the first pair of things go together. Use the word bank to complete the sentence and make the second pair of things go together **in the same way** as the first pair.

1.   Bee is to sting as cat is to_____ .

2.   Pancakes are to fry as cake is to _____ .

3.   State is to Ohio as city is to _____ .

4.   Horse is to colt as bear is to _____ .

5.   Herd is to sheep as flock is to _____ .

6.   Hen is to seed as horse is to _____ .

7.   Walk is to slow as jump is to _____ .

8.   Tadpole is to frog as caterpillar is to _____ .

wolf	Boston	butterfly	high
bake	California	cocoon	birds
hay	cub	barn	scratch

Think about how the first two things in each sentence go together. Then fill in the blanks with two more things that go together **in the same way.**

1. Calf is to cow as _____ is to _____ .

2. King is to castle as_____ is to_____ .

3. Circle is to round as _____ is to _____ .

4. Eyes are to see as_____ is to_____ .

5. Drive is to car as _____ is to _____ .

6. Dog is to "Woof" as _____ is to _____ .

7. Hat is to head as _____ is to _____ .

8. Fish is to water as _____ is to _____ .

Match each set of directions to the correct box. Write the letter next to the box. The first one is done for you.

1

A. Circle the money and cross out the animals.

2

B. Cross out the things that are not alive.

3

C. Circle the animals and put a line under the money.

4

D. Circle the things that are alive.

5

E. Circle the thing that can fly.

Match each set of directions to the correct box. Write the letter next to the box.

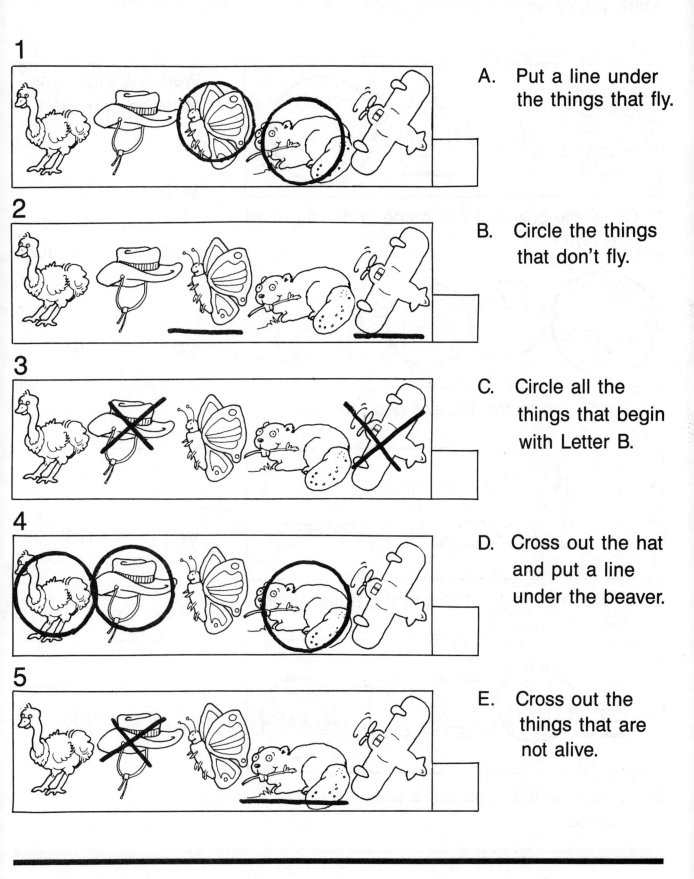

1

A. Put a line under the things that fly.

2

B. Circle the things that don't fly.

3

C. Circle all the things that begin with Letter B.

4

D. Cross out the hat and put a line under the beaver.

5

E. Cross out the things that are not alive.

Read the directions for each row. Have they been followed correctly?
Mark yes or no.

Were the directions
followed correctly?

yes   no

1. Circle the cow and put a line under the food
   she gives.

yes   no

2. Circle the foods that are good for you.

yes   no

3. Cross out the top hat and put a line under
   letter D.

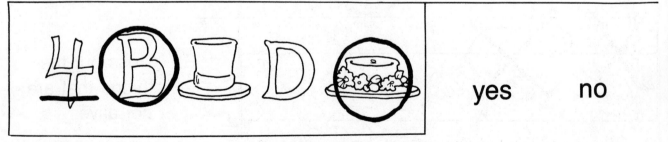

yes   no

4. Circle the hats and put a line under the
   number.

Read the directions for each row. Have they been followed correctly?
Mark yes or no.

Were the directions
followed correctly?

yes   no

1.   Circle the things that begin with letter H.

yes   no

2.   Put a line under the things that live in water
     and circle the number.

yes   no

3.   Cross out the things that rhyme.

yes   no

4.   Cross out the two things that live in water and
     put a line under the opposite of thin.

The computer mixed up two stories! Each story is in the right order, but both are tangled together. On the next page copy each story as it should be.

The King loved to cook. Mary was a happy witch. He baked a chocolate cake for the Queen. He began to carry the huge cake into the royal dining room. But Mrs. Noseup, who lived next door, was not happy. Then the King slipped! She did not like living next door to a witch. One night Mary heard Mrs. Noseup scream. The cake fell all over the Queen. A robber was tying up Mrs. Noseup. The Queen just laughed. Mary turned the robber into a toad. Now Mrs. Noseup is happy to have a witch next door. "I love upside-down cake," she said.

When you have finished untangling the stories, write a title for each one.

Story 1: _____

_____

_____

_____

_____

_____

_____

_____

Story 2: _____

_____

_____

_____

_____

_____

_____

_____

_____

Here's a limerick for you:

> There was a young lady named May,
> Who liked to watch TV all day.
> She stayed in her bed,
> And sat there like lead,
> Till her Mom threw the TV away!

Below are two mixed-up limericks. You must sort them out and put them in the right order. Look at the next page. The first line of each one is done for you.

There was an old witch named Elaine,

She washed once a year,

Who thought being a king was a bore.

And put money down

She won't even go out in the rain!

There was a king from Baltimore,

Who thought taking a bath was a pain.

And from what I hear,

He gave up his crown,

To open a grocery store!

The first line of each limerick is done for you. When you are done, write a title for each one.

There was an old witch named Elaine,

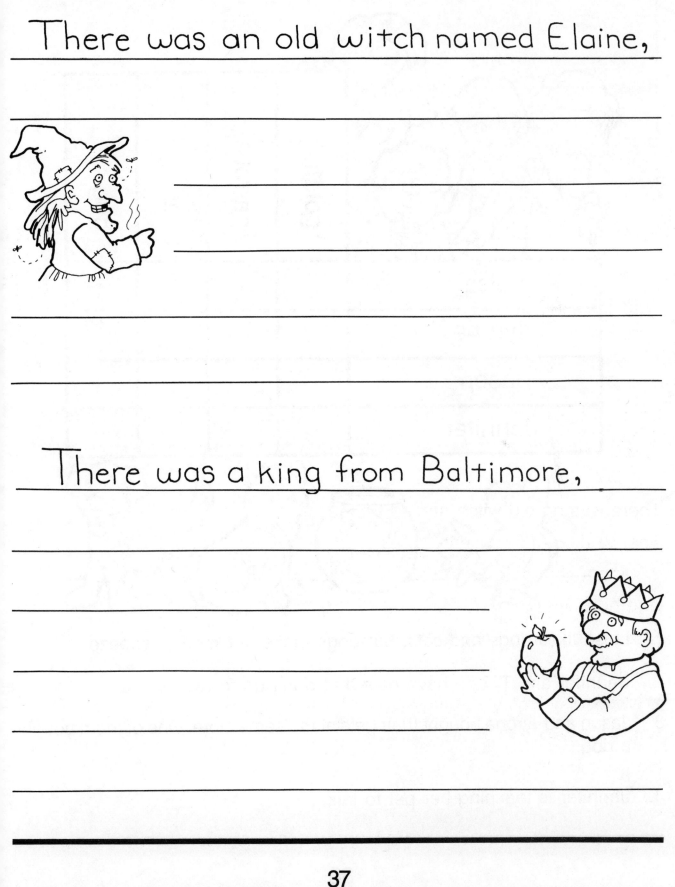

There was a king from Baltimore,

Four friends have pets. Read all the clues. Then mark the chart with X's to match each pet with its owner.

	goldfish	parrot	cat	dog
Luisa				
Tyrone				
Jason				
Jennifer				

1. Luisa likes dogs and cats, but dogs make her mother sneeze.

2. Jennifer and Tyrone have pets that don't go for walks.

3. Jason and Tyrone bought their pets at the same store. One of them bought a dog.

4. Jennifer is teaching her pet to talk.

It's spring cleaning at the Rogers' house! Read all the clues. Then mark the chart with X's to match each person with his job.

	Barry	Tom	Sherry	Alyson	Wayne
Wash the windows					
Sweep the floors					
Dust the attic					
Trim the trees					
Paint the door					

1. Tom was the only one who used soap and water.

2. Wayne needed a ladder and clippers.

3. Sherry did not dust.

4. Barry swept the floor.

5. Alyson did not paint.

Every hippo helped get ready for Wanda's tea party. Read all the clues. Then mark the chart with X's to show what each hippo did.

	plates	cups	tea	cake
Wanda				
Ellie				
Rex				
Ralph				

1. Wanda brewed the tea.

2. Someone brought the cups.

3. Rex hates to cook, but Ralph loves to bake.

4. Ellie remembered the plates.

Four children rode to the park. Read all the clues. Then make X's on the chart to match the children with the things they rode to the park.

	Dale	Bonnie	Anna	Bert
skateboard				
bike				
roller skates				
scooter				

1. Dale loves to ride his bike.

2. Dale lives across the street from the person with the skateboard.

3. Bert lives next door to Dale.

4. Bonnie just got her new scooter.

Read all the clues. Then fill in the chart to show which candy each person ate.

	Sara	Milo	Ed	Drew	Ali	Rose
raisin						
jelly						
vanilla						
cherry						
fudge						
peanut						

1. Sara hates raisins.

2. Milo ate a candy that was white inside.

3. Ed ate the fudge or the peanut.

4. Drew always loves what his sister Sara hates.

5. Ali ate the peanut.

6. Rose loves fruit flavors.

Try to solve this puzzle. Read everything first! Then write your answers.

1. Tony bought toys for his brother and his two sisters.

2. He bought a ball, a game, and a coloring book.

3. Amy does not like games, and Tony did not give her the ball.

4. Mark likes everything, and Tracy doesn't like to play ball.

Amy got the _____ .

Mark got the _____ .

Tracy got the _____ .

Read all the clues first. Then think carefully and write the answers to this puzzle. What does each parrot say.?

1. Luis taught his three parrots to talk.

2. He taught them to say "Hello," "Wow," and "Stop."

3. Sukie cannot say "Stop," and Luis did not teach her to say "Wow."

4. Luis did not teach Pookie to say "Stop."

Sukie   Flookie   Pookie

Here's a puzzle for experts! Read everything before you answer. Then write the name of each turtle in its correct place.

1. Four turtles had a race.

2. Luke got to the Finish Line in six days, and Lulu got there sooner.

3. Harry finished behind Lulu and in front of Luke.

4. Jenny got to the Finish Line before Lulu.

Who won? _____

Who came in last? _____

45

Page 4: His name is Alan.

Page 5: The thief is Max.

Page 6: A. Alana   B. Leesa   C. Carol   D. Joyce
E. Helen

Page 7: A. Susan   B. Mary   C. Jill   D. Maria
E. Yolanda   F. Hilary

Page 8: A. Carl   B. Willy   C. Sophia   D. Adam
E. Mike   F. Sherry   G. Tony

Page 9: 1-b, 2-c, 3-a, 4-b

Page 10: 1-b, 2-a, 3-c, 4-a

Page 11: 1-C, 2-C, 3-D, 4-A, 5-C

Page 12: 1-B, 2-C, 3-D, 4-A, 5-B

Page 13: 1-C, 2-B, 3-A, 4-B, 5-C

Page 14: 1-B, 2-A, 3-C, 4-B, 5-C

Page 15:

Page 16: 1. boots   2. walked   3. yellow   4. boat
5. ice   6. melted   7. ✔   8. barked

Page 17: 1. capital   2. hear   3. glad   4. talked   5. ✔
6. wasn't   7. great   8. smell

Page 18: 1. lost   2. deaf   3. start   4. ✔   5. soaked
6. baseball   7. closes   8. hat

Page 19: 5-A, 3-B, 1-C, 4-D, 2-E

Page 20: 5-A, 3-B, 6-C, 2-D, 1-E, 4-F

Page 21: Red: A-3, B-1, C-2
Wolf: A-1, B-3, C-2

Page 22: Sam: A-3, B-4, C-1, D-2
Dan: A-3, B-4, C-2, D-1

Page 23: 2. colors　3. fruits　4. buildings　5. sports
6. machines　7. tools　8. babies　9. girls
10. storms

Page 24: 1. white　2. fly　3. go around　4. grow
5. countries　6. cities　7. open　8. seasons
9. boys　10. light

Page 25: Answers will vary.

Page 26: Answers will vary.

Page 27: 2. cat　3. foot　4. barn　5. June　6. garage
7. flower　8. eat

Page 28: 1. scratch　2. bake　3. Boston　4. cub
5. birds　6. hay　7. high　8. butterfly

Page 29: Answers will vary.

Page 30: 1-C, 2-E, 3-A, 4-B, 5-D

Page 31: 1-C, 2-A, 3-E, 4-B, 5-D

Page 32: 1. yes　2. no　3. no　4. no

Page 33: 1. no　2. yes　3. no　4. no

Page 35: The King loved to cook. He baked a chocolate cake for the Queen. He began to carry the cake into the royal dining room. Then the King slipped! The cake fell all over the Queen. The Queen just laughed. "I love upside-down cake," she said.

Mary was a happy witch. But Mrs. Noseup, who lived next door, was not happy. She did not like living next door to a witch. One night Mary heard Mrs. Noseup scream. A robber was tying up Mrs. Noseup. Mary turned the robber into a toad. Now Mrs. Noseup is happy to have a witch next door.

Page 37: There was an old witch named Elaine,
Who thought taking a bath was a pain.
She washed once a year,
And from what I hear,
She won't even go out in the rain.

There was a King from Baltimore,
Who thought being a king was a bore.
He gave up his crown,
And put money down
To open a grocery store!

Page 38: Luisa: cat,   Tyrone: goldfish,   Jason: dog,
Jennifer: parrot

Page 39: Barry: sweep floor,   Tom: wash windows,
Sherry: paint,   Alyson: dust,   Wayne: trim trees

Page 40: Wanda: tea,   Ellie: plates,   Rex: cups,
Ralph: cake

Page 41: Dale: bike,   Bonnie: scooter,   Anna: skateboard
Bert: roller skates

Page 42: Sara: jelly,   Milo: vanilla,   Ed: fudge,
Drew: raisin,   Ali: peanut,   Rose: cherry

Page 43: Amy got the coloring book;   Mark got the ball;
Tracy got the game.

Page 44: Sukie says: "Hello";   Flookie says: "Stop";
Pookie says: "Wow."

Page 45: Jenny won.   Luke came in last.